KT-494-098

THE FUNNIEST FOOTBALL JOKE BOOK EVER!

Collect them all!

The Funniest Animal Joke Book Ever

The Funniest Back to School Joke Book Ever

The Funniest Christmas Joke Book Ever

The Funniest Dinosaur Joke Book Ever

The Funniest Holiday Joke Book Ever

The Funniest Space Joke Book Ever

The Funniest Spooky Joke Book Ever

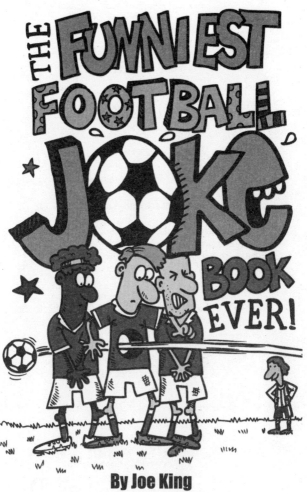

THE FUNNIEST FOOTBALL JOKE BOOK EVER!

By Joe King

Illustrated by Nigel Baines

Andersen Press

This edition first published in Great Britain in 2016 by
Andersen Press Limited
20 Vauxhall Bridge Road, London SW1V 2SA, UK
Vijverlaan 48, 3062 HL Rotterdam, Nederland

www.andersenpress.co.uk

Text copyright © Andersen Press Ltd., 2010, 2016
Illustrations copyright © Nigel Baines, 2010

6 8 10 9 7

All rights reserved. No part of this publication may be
reproduced, stored in a retrieval system or transmitted
in any form, or by any means, electronic, mechanical,
photocopying, recording or otherwise, without the
written permission of the publisher.

The moral right of the illustrator has been asserted.

British Library Cataloguing in
Publication Data available.

ISBN 978 1 84939 111 5

Printed and bound in Great Britain
by Clays Ltd, Elcograf S.p.A.

WORLD CUP
FEVER

Why did the winning
team spin their
trophy round
and round?
*It was the
Whirled Cup.*

Gareth Southgate won't stand for any nonsense. Last week he caught a couple of England fans climbing over the wall at Wembley. He was furious. He grabbed them by the collar and said, 'Now get back in there and watch the game till it finishes.'

Which English footballer is always in debt?
Michael Owing.

**How does Gareth Southgate
drive to work?**
In a 4x4x2.

**What will Gareth Southgate
do if the pitch is flooded?**
Bring on his subs.

**Which Brazilian star forgot
where he parked his Mercedes?**
Roberto Car-loss.

**Which English footballer do
you need when you've
got a cold?**
Rachel Yankey-chief

**Why did no-one visit the
nightclub owned by Diego Costa?**
It was a dive.

Three old football fans are in church, praying for their teams.

The first one asks, 'Oh Lord, when will Spurs win the Premiership?'

God replies, 'In the next five years.'

'But I'll be dead by then,' says the man.

The second one asks, 'Oh Lord, when will Everton win the FA Cup?'

God replies, 'In the next ten years.'

'But I'll be dead by then,' says the old fan.

The third one asks, 'Oh Lord, when will England win the World Cup again?'

God answers, '*I'll* be dead by then.'

What are Brazilian fans called?
Brazil nuts.

What comes from Central America, has 100,000 hands and whizzes round the football stadium?
A Mexican wave.

FOOTBALLING FUNNIES

**Which part of a football pitch
smells the nicest?**
The scenter spot.

**Why aren't football stadiums
built in outer space?**
There's no atmosphere.

**What is Jordan Nobbs'
favourite biscuit?**
Hob-Nobbs

**Why are footballers
like magicians?**
They can both do hat tricks.

Do grasshoppers watch football?
No, they prefer cricket.

**What do you get if you cross
martial arts with soccer?**
Kung fu-tball.

**Why are football directors'
meetings so dull?**
They're held in the bored room.

**Whose job is it to carry the
players to each match?**
The coach.

**Why did the striker play in his
living room?**
It was a home game.

**Why do footballers
carry hankies?**
Because they're always dribbling.

**What type of footballer is
best at lighting a match?**
A striker.

**What do you call a girl who
stands at the end of the pitch
and catches the ball?**
Annette.

Why was the pitch waterlogged?
Because players kept dribbling on it.

Why did the football pitch become a triangle?
Someone took a corner.

**Why did the footballer jump
over a rope in the middle
of the match?**
She was the skipper.

**What does Gary Lineker always
order in restaurants?**
Catch of the Day.

**What's the angriest
part of the goal?**
The crossbar.

**Why is it easy to predict the
weather after a football game?**
*There are always showers
after the match.*

**What happened when
the footballer ran out of salt
and pepper in May?**
It was the end of the seasoning.

**Why couldn't the car
play football?**
It only had one boot.

**Which part of a football ground
never stays the same?**
The changing rooms.

**Why did Wayne Rooney take
cheese to the England
training session?**
*He heard Gareth was going to give
him a free role.*

**Why was the football
stadium so chilly?**
It was full of fans.

**What bounds across
Australia scoring great goals?**
A kangarooney.

What did the ref say to the chicken who tripped a defender?
Fowl.

Did you hear about the footballer who wore too much aftershave?
He was scent off.

What's a footballer's favourite dessert?
Pitch Melba.

**Why did the footballer
stay on the pavement?**
Because he was an awful crosser.

**Why did the player cry
when he was transferred
to another team?**
Because he was moved.

What do footballers drink?
Penal-tea.

**Did you hear about the time it
was raining football players?**
It was teaming down.

**Who can spot a good player at
the same time as lighting a fire?**
A scout.

Did you hear about the footballer whose bad habits rubbed off on the other players?
He was a transfer.

Where do footballers go if they want to become film stars?
Volleywood.

What sort of grass do aliens play football on?
Astroturf.

**Why does the team of artists
never win?**
They like to draw.

**Why was Cinderella
bad at football?**
Because she ran away from the ball.

**What did the millionaire
caveman own?**
His own club.

**Why was the footballer
upset on his birthday?**
He got a red card.

**What has 22 legs, 11 heads, 2
wings and goes crunch?**
A football team eating crisps.

**Why was the centipede dropped
from the football team?**
*Because he took too long
putting his boots on.*

**What did the owl say
at the football match?**
There's a twit or two.

Knock Knock.
Who's there?
Football.
Football who?
Football hooligan.

Why can't dogs play football?
They have two left feet.

Why do fairy godmothers make great football coaches?
Because they always help you get to the ball.

Why are babies great at football?
Because they're always dribbling.

**In which league do
fried potatoes play?**
The Premierchip.

**Who scored the most goals in
the Greek Mythology league?**
The Centaur forward.

**Why didn't the dog
play football?**
Because it was a boxer.

**Why did a couple of
young cows chase a ball
round a football pitch?**
It was a game of two calves.

**Why did the bird flap along the
side of the pitch?**
It was a winger.

**What did the
footballing bee say?**
Hive scored!

**Why are there no football
matches in the zoo?**
There are too many cheetahs.

It was mid-way through
the football season and a
school team was doing really
badly. The coach decided to get
the team together and
go through some basics.
Picking up a football he said,
'Right lads, what I have in
my hand is a football and
the object of the game is to . . .'
'Hang on a minute,' came a
shout, 'you're going too fast.'

Who is Chewbacca's favourite footballer?
Mia Hamm Solo

TV Commentator:
So why are you retiring?
Player:
Well basically it's a question of illness and fatigue.
TV Commentator:
Can you be more specific?
Player:
Well specifically the fans are sick and tired of me.

'I've been watching you play and I might be able to help you.'
'Great. Thanks. Are you a coach?'
'No, I'm an optician.'

What do baby footballers wear?
Bibs.

Why did the footballer hold his boot to his ear?
He liked sole music.

Why didn't the nose make the school football team?
It wasn't picked.

Why did the footballer take her pencil to bed?
She wanted to draw the curtains.

Where do footballers dance?
At a foot-ball.

**How do chickens encourage
their football teams?**
They egg them on.

'I thought you said he eats,
drinks and sleeps football!'
'He does. He just can't play it.'

Why did the stupid footballer wear his shirt in the bath?
Because it said wash and wear.

Why did the stupid footballer sleep with a banana skin under his pillow?
So he could slip out of bed in the morning.

**Did you hear about the
football player who ate a candle
before a game?**
He wanted a light snack.

**Pessimists see the cup half
empty and optimists see
it half full. My team
hasn't even seen the cup.**

What did the footballer say when he accidentally burped during a game?
Sorry, it was a freak hic.

Why was the goalpost angry?
Because the bar was rattled.

What is a bank manager's favourite type of football?
Fiver-a-side.

What did they call Dracula when he won the league?
The Champire.

Old football players never die, they just pass away.

Two boys were at a football match and it was just seconds away from kick off. 'I'm bursting for a wee,' said the first boy, 'and the toilets are miles away.'

'Don't worry,' said the second boy. 'You see that man in front of you? Just wee up his leg.'

'Are you crazy, that man's massive!'

'Oh, he won't notice anything.'

'How d'you know?'

'Because I've just weed up yours.'

A thick fan arrives at a football match during the second half. 'What's the score?' he asks.
'Nil-nil.'
'And what was the score at half time?'

First fan:
I wish I'd brought the piano to the match.

Second fan:
Why would you bring a piano?

First fan:
Because I left the tickets on it.

'We've got the best team in the country. Unbeaten and no goals scored against us.'
'How many games have you played?'
'The first one's on Saturday.'

Little Jack Horner
Once took a corner,
And belted the ball so high.
With the Keeper upset
It went straight in the net,
And he said,
'What a good boy am I!'

Why did the footballer throw his watch out the window?
He wanted to see time fly.

How do footballers stay cool?
They stand next to the fans.

For a minute we were
in with a chance.
And then the game started.

They beat us six-nothing. And
we were lucky to get nothing.

Some flies were playing football
in a saucer, using a sugar lump
as a ball. One of them said, 'We'll
have to do better than this, lads,
we're in the cup tomorrow.'

COME ON, REF!

If you have a referee in football,
what do you have in bowls?
Cereal.

Ref: I'm sending you off.
Player: What for?
Ref: For the rest of the match.

**'We're starting up a football
team. Would you like to join?'**
*'I would, but I don't know the first
thing about football.'*
**'That's OK, we're looking for a
referee as well.'**

A spectator at a match kept shouting insults at the referee. Eventually the referee had had enough and marched over to the noisy fan and shouted, 'Look here, I've been watching you for the last twenty minutes.'
'I thought so,' the fan shouted back. 'I knew you couldn't have been watching the game.'

Football player:
If I call you rude names will you send me off?

Ref:
Of course.

Player:
But you can't send me off for thinking them?

Ref:
No.

Player:
*Well then I think you're a ****** *******!*

**Humpty Dumpty sat on the wall.
So the ref booked him.**

**Why did the ref
snap her watch in two?**
It was half time.

**How do you know if a ref is
enjoying his job?**
He whistles while he works.

MANAGER MAYHEM!

Why were the two managers sitting around sketching china?
It was a cup draw.

Manager:
If you don't pay attention, I'll give you a piece of my mind.

Player:
Are you sure you can spare it, boss?

Manager:
*How did you miss
training yesterday?*

Player:
I didn't miss it one bit.

Manager:
*You've got your football boots
on the wrong feet.*

Player:
They're the only feet I've got.

Manager:
I wish you'd pay a little attention.

Player:
*I'm paying as little
attention as I can.*

Manager:
I've just had a brilliant idea.

Coach:
It's probably beginner's luck.

Manager:
*I thought I told you
to lose weight. What happened
to your two week diet?*

Player:
I finished it in two days.

Manager:
*Is your poor performance down
to ignorance or apathy?*

Player:
I don't know and I don't care.

Manager:
*Our new player cost ten million.
I call him our wonder player.*

Fan:
Why's that?

Manager:
*Because every time I see him play
I wonder why I bought him.*

Manager:
I'll give you a thousand pounds a week to start with and two thousand a week in a year's time.

Player:
OK, I'll come back in a year's time.

Player:
I could kick myself for missing that goal.

Manager:
Don't bother, you'd probably miss.

Player:
I've just seen the doctor and he says I can't play football.

Manager:
Oh, he's seen you play too, has he?

Striker:
I've just had an idea for strengthening the team.

Manager:
Good, when are you leaving?

LOONY LIMERICKS

There was a young player called Wayne,
Who caused the defenders some pain.
He scored lots of goals,
Far more than Paul Scholes,
So that's why he gets all the fame.

A young player who always played rough
Faced a ref who was terribly tough.
He tackled too hard,
And was shown the red card,
With the comment 'Enough is enough'.

There was a young player called Rick,
Who was known for the strength of his kick.
With the ball on the spot,
He took a short trot,
And the goalie felt hit with a brick.

There once was a very good goalie,
Whose weakness was Mum's ravioli.
His waistline expanded,
He became heavy handed,
And played like a slow roly poly.

PUFF
WHEEZE

There was a young groundsman from Leeds,
Who swallowed a packet of seeds.
Within the hour,
His head was in flower,
And he couldn't sit down for the weeds.

A striker from somewhere in Kent,
Took free kicks which dipped and then bent.
In a match on the telly,
He gave one some welly,
And the keeper the wrong way he sent.

There was a young striker from Spain,
Who hated to play in the rain.
One day in a muddle,
He stepped in a puddle,
And got washed away down a drain.

A player who turned out for Dover,
Had no shirt so wore a pullover.
But the thing was too long,
And he put it on wrong,
So that all he could do was fall over.

A footballing legend called Paul,
Did fabulous things with a ball.
In one of his tricks,
With a series of flicks,
He managed to knock down a brick wall.

A striker who came from Devizes,
Did little to help win the prizes.
When asked for a reason,
He said, 'Well this season,
My boots were of two different sizes.'

TEAM
TEASERS!

**What is black and white
and black and white and
black and white?**
A Newcastle fan rolling down a hill.

**Which is the chilliest ground in
the Premiership?**
Cold Trafford.

**What's the difference between
an Arsenal fan and a coconut?**
*One's thick and hairy.
The other's a tropical fruit.*

**Which team is never introduced
to each other before matches?**
Queens Park Strangers.

**Which football team
loves ice cream?**
Aston Vanilla.

**Why don't Norwich City
make much money from
selling players?**
Because canaries go cheap.

**What's claret and blue
and delicious?**
A West Ham sandwich.

**What is the bluest sea
in the world?**
The Chelsea.

Fire swept through a library at
The Kop last night, destroying
thousands of books. A firefighter
said the real tragedy was that
many of them had not even been
coloured in yet.

**What's the difference between a
Man United fan and a chimp?**
*One's hairy, stupid and smells.
The other is a monkey.*

GOALIE GAGS

How does a keeper send his Christmas cards?
By goal post.

Did you hear about the goalie with the huge piggy bank?
He was always saving.

Did you hear about the useless goalkeeper?
When he missed a save on Saturday he put his head in his hands – and dropped it!

Oi, Stupid, OVER HERE!

**Which goalkeeper can jump
higher than a crossbar?**
They all can. Crossbars can't jump.

**What is a goalkeeper's
favourite snack?**
Beans on post.

**Mary had a little lamb
Who played in goal a lot.
It let the ball go through its legs
So now it's in the pot.**

**What position did
the ghost play?**
Ghoulie.

CHEEKY
FOOTBALL
CHANTS

**'Oh my God I can't believe it,
We've never been this good
away from home!'**
*Leeds fans to the tune of Kaiser
Chiefs' **Oh My God***

'It's a hard knock life for us,
It's a hard knock life for us,
Instead of Brendan, we get Klopp,
Instead of nowhere, we'll get top!
It's a hard knock life!'

Liverpool fans improvise to the tune of
It's a Hard Knock Life *from Annie*

'You put your whole self in, your
whole self out,
In out, in out, you shake it all about,
You do the Dele Alli,
And you turn around,
That's what it's all about!
Ahhhhh Dele Alli (x3)
Knees bent, arms stretched ra ra ra!'

Spurs fans to tune of the **Hokey
Cokey**

'Soooo Vardy is great,
You know it's too late
when he's walking on by.
He scores every game,
But don't look back in anger,
Because he's great.'

Leicester fans to the tune of Oasis hit
Don't Look Back in Anger

**'Juan love,
Juan heart,
Pass the ball to Mata
And we will be all right.'**

*Manchester United fans to the tune
of Bob Marley's **One Love***

**'So here's to you, Ashley Williams,
Everton loves you more than you will
know. Wo-oh oh!'**

*Everton fans sing another
version of Simon and
Garfunkel's **Mrs Robinson***

'Wilf Zaha, Zaha,
Whatever you'll be, you'll be,
You took us to Wembley,
Wilf Zaha, Zaha.'

Crystal Palace fans with their own
version of **Que Sera Sera**
(Whatever Will Be, Will Be)

'Hey, I'm a left back,
And this is crazy,
But I just scored a goal, so call me Bainsey!
And all the other clubs,
Try to sign me,
But I just scored a goal, so call me Bainsey!'

Everton fans pay tribute to the tune of
Call Me Maybe *(Carly Rae Jepson)*

'Hey ho, his name is Mo,
He's a little bit tall with a massive afro,
He's mates with Pienaar and Darron Gibbo,
His second name's Fellaini!'

Manchester United fans to the tune of
Robbie Williams' **Candy**

THE FUNNIEST BACK TO SCHOOL JOKE BOOK EVER

JOE KING

Why did the school bully kick the classroom computer? **Someone told him he was supposed to boot up the system**

Why did the boy come first in the 100-metre sprint? **He had athlete's foot**

Dinner lady: Eat up your greens, they are good for your skin!
Pupil: But I don't want green skin!

These and many more hilarious jokes will keep everyone chortling at playtime!

9781849395779

THE FUNNIEST SPOOKY JOKE BOOK EVER

JOE KING

What happens if you see twin witches? **You won't be able to tell which witch is witch**

What did the skeleton say when his brother told a lie? **You can't fool me, I can see right through you**

What's a ghost's favourite party game? **Hide-and-shriek**

These and many more howlers will make you laugh your head off (in most cases not literally).

9781849393010

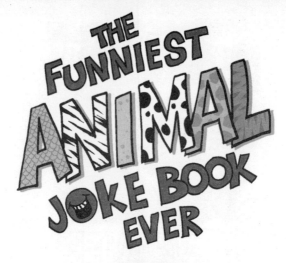

THE FUNNIEST ANIMAL JOKE BOOK EVER

JOE KING

What do you call a pig who knows karate?
Pork chop

What is black, white and red all over?
A sunburnt penguin

What do you call an elephant in
a phone booth?
Stuck

You'll fall out of your tree
laughing at these rib-tickling
animal jokes!

9781783442331